# *The Logomachía*

John Apocalypse

with Chabril Bar Yaqoub

ISBN #: 978-1-312-37736-3

# <u>Table of Contents</u>

# **<u>Introduction</u>**

May be the most striking thing in this book is its title,

"Logomachia". It is composed of two parts, logo and machia

meaning strife of words or dispute over the meaning of words.

In fact the word, any word, is not just a group of letters but it is

a symbol of a specific concept. Every group of concepts

constitutes altogether a specific dogma. Therefore any dispute

over words is actually a dispute over a precious concept that

lies behind that word and that compose a valuable dogma.

Dogmas, in their turns, should be neither the fruit of a mere

deductive thinking nor a group of hypotheses and theories

engendered by human logical thinking. They are rather

inspired facts and truths by the Holy Spirit about Whom Jesus

said, "When He, the Spirit of truth has come, He will guide

you into all truth" (John16:13).

Therefore any ecumenical movement should not be built on a

mere narcissistic attempt to prove that one's denomination is the only owner and defender of the absolute truth. In fact, whoever wants to pursue this absolute truth must be first guided by and filled with the Holy Spirit.

This book is based on a single verse in the Holy Bible, "And the disciples were first called Christians in Antioch" (Acts11:26). The author used, in a marvelous way, this single verse as a keystone reference to all his biblical and historical arguments about the pastoral tradition, the church authority and the Sacraments which constitute, among others, three fundamental doctrines of the dogma of the Orthodox Church.

May the Holy Spirit bless the words of truth present in this book as well as his author who is full of zeal; and "He who has an ear, let him hear what the Spirit says to the churches" (Revelation2:7).


Bishop Youssef,

Bishop of the Coptic Orthodox Diocese of the Southern United States

# **What is an Apostolic Father**

Before we start we should define what an apostolic father is. "The Apostolic Fathers, Christian writers of the first and second centuries who are known, or are considered, to have had personal relations with some of the Apostles, or to have been so influenced by them that their writings may be held as echoes of genuine Apostolic teaching. Though restricted by some to those who were actually disciples of the Apostles, the term applies by extension to certain writers who were previously believed to have been such, and virtually embraces all the remains of primitive Christian literature antedating the great apologies of the second century, and forming the link of tradition that binds these latter writings to those of the New Testament...The period of time covered by these writings extends from the last two decades of the first century for the Didache (80-100), Clement (c. 97), and probably Pseudo-Barnabas (96-98), through the first half of the second century, the approximate chronology being Ignatius, 110-117; Polycarp, 110-120; Hermas, in its present form, c. 150; Papias, c.150. Geographically, Rome is represented by Clement and Hermas; Polycarp wrote from Smyrna, whence also Ignatius sent four of the seven epistles which he wrote on his way from Antioch through Asia Minor; Papias was Bishop of Hierapolis in Phrygia; the Didache was written in Egypt or Syria; the letter of Barnabas in Alexandria."1

# St. Ignatius of Antioch

How do we define what is Christian? With many denominations, one differing from the next, all claiming to be Christian how are we to know for sure which one is and which one is not. Certainly two vastly different denominations cannot both at the same time be Christian while differing in nearly every way. Where should our starting point in defining Christianity be? We must all agree that scripture should be the starting point as protestants base their authority entirely in scripture it would only be fair to them to start there. Therefore we must find in scripture where the term Christian is first used and then seek how that term is defined. Acts 11:26 tells us that: "And the disciples were first called Christians in Antioch." Logic says it all, whatever was there in Antioch is what we should consider Christian. The disciples laid their foundations there and logically speaking those foundations would have to be considered Christian.

It just so happens that we have writings from Antioch during the time of the apostles. St. Ignatius of Antioch was taught by the apostles and ordained bishop of Antioch by them as well. It stands to reason that his writings would more closely resemble the teachings of the apostles than, say, Martin Luther or some other modern day teacher. Having been taught by St. John the Apostle gives some authority to the writings of St. Ignatius, as again, they would logically more closely reflect apostolic teaching than someone who came much later. Therefore whatever the letters of St. Ignatius might say is likely what he was taught directly and of course the letters do not likely contain everything he was taught they should give us an idea, at the very least, of the definition of Christian.

St. Ignatius touches on a few key points that really demonstrate what Christian really means, he stresses some points several times in his letters, namely the hierarchal structure of the church and the necessity of the bishop. He mentions the sacraments and the nature of Christ as well. Now we will look at some excerpts that really give us a clue as to what St. Ignatius considered to be Christian.

## Bishops and Doctrines

"In the same way all should respect the deacons as they would Jesus Christ, just as they respect the bishop as representing the Father and the priests the council of God and the college of the apostles. Apart from these there is nothing that can be called a church." (*Letter to the Trallians, Ch. 2*)

"Anyone who is within the sanctuary is pure and anyone who is outside is impure, that is to say, no one who acts apart from the bishop and the priests and the deacons has a clear conscience." (*Letter to the Trallians, Ch. 7*)

"For, all who belong to God and Jesus Christ are with the bishop. And those, too, will belong to God who have returned, repentant, to the unity of the church so as to live in accordance with Jesus Christ. Make no mistake, brethren, no one who follows another into schism inherits the kingdom of God. No one who follows heretical doctrine is on the side of the passion." (*Letter to the Philadelphians, Ch. 3*)

"Shun schisms, as the source of troubles. Let all follow the bishop as Jesus Christ did the Father, and the priests, as you would the apostles. Reverence the deacons as you would the command of God. Apart from the bishop, let no one perform any of the functions that pertain to the church. Let that

Eucharist be held valid which is offered by the bishop or by one to whom the bishop has committed this charge. Where the bishop appears, there let the people be; as wherever Jesus Christ is, there is the Catholic (universal) Church. It is not lawful to baptize or give communion without the consent of the bishop. Thus, whatever is done will be safe and valid." (*Letter to the Smyrnaeans, Ch. 8*)

"For wherever there is division or anger, God has no place. Now God forgives all who repent, so long as their repentance turns to union with God and to communion with the bishop." (*Letter to the Philadelphians, Ch. 8*)

"Make no mistake brethren; the corrupters of families will not inherit the kingdom of God. If, then, those who are dead who do these things according to the flesh, how much worse if, with bad doctrine, one should corrupt the faith of God for which Jesus Christ was crucified. Such a man, for becoming contaminated, will depart into unquenchable fire; and will

anyone who listens to him." (*Letter to the Ephesians, Ch. 16*

## Sacraments

"The docetics abstain from the Eucharist and from prayer,

because they do not admit that the Eucharist is the flesh of our

Savior Jesus Christ, the flesh which suffered for our sins and

which the Father, in His graciousness, raised from the dead.

And so denying the gift of God, these men perish in their

disputatiousness. It would be better for them to love and so to

rise again. It is well for you to keep away from such persons

and not even to speak of them in private or in public. It is

better to keep to the prophets and especially to the Gospel in

which the passion is presented and the resurrection is an

accomplished fact." (*Letter to the Smyrnaeans, Ch. 6*)


"I desire the bread of God, the Heavenly Bread, the Bread of

Life, which is the flesh of Jesus Christ, the Son of God, who

became afterwards the seed of David and Abraham; I wish the

drink of God, namely His Blood, which is incorruptible love and eternal life." (*Letter to the Romans, Ch. 7*)

Upon reading these few passages we can conclude that St. Ignatius believed in the importance of the clergy, even stating that without it a church cannot be considered a church. He also stresses the importance of the sacrament of the Eucharist, stating clearly that this sacrament is the body and blood of our Lord and Savior Jesus Christ. This destroys the notion that the Eucharist is merely symbolic and shows that the early church, where they were called Christian, teaches that this sacrament *is* the body and blood of Jesus Christ. Therefore if someone were to come along later and teach opposite of these teachings, it would have to be considered bad doctrine. St. Ignatius tells us in his letter to the Ephesians that if one, with bad doctrine, should corrupt the faith of God, he will depart into unquenchable fire. He also says of those that follow another into schism does not inherit the kingdom of God.

# St. Clement of Rome

*"And I intreat thee also, true yokefellow, help those women which laboured with me in the gospel, with Clement also, and with other my fellow labourers, whose names are in the book of life."* Phillippians 4:3

Here we see St. Paul mentioning a Clement in the above said verse, but who exactly is this Clement? Origen identifies Pope Clement with St. Paul's fellow-labourer, Philippians 4:2-3 and so do Eusebius, Epiphanius, and Jerome.[2] According to Tertullian, writing c. 199, the Roman Church claimed that Clement was ordained by St. Peter (*De Praescript., xxxii*), and St. Jerome tells us that in his time "most of the Latins" held that Clement was the immediate successor of the Apostle. (*De viris illustr., xv*) Now, since St. Clement was a contemporary of the apostles, and likely taught as well as ordained by them, his word too should also enlighten us as to what it is to be a Christian. What he teaches also should not differ in any way to St. Ignatius of Antioch thereby showing consistency of a true church.

## Church Authority

Starting with Clement of Rome, in his letter to the Corinthians, he writes: "The apostles received the gospel for us from the Lord Jesus Christ; Jesus Christ was sent from God. Christ, therefore is from God and the apostles from Christ. Both, accordingly, came in proper order by the will of God. Receiving their orders, therefore, and being filled with confidence because of the resurrection of the Lord Jesus Christ, and confirmed in the word of God, with full assurance of the Holy Spirit, they went forth preaching the gospel of the kingdom of God that was about to come. Preaching, accordingly, throughout the country and the cities, they appointed their first fruits, after testing them by the spirit, to be bishops and deacons of those who should believe." (*Letter to the Corinthians, Ch.42*)

Clement is speaking of preaching the gospel or good news of the kingdom of God. He does not say anything about being taught by scripture alone. Clement speaks about the authority of the church and her appointed leaders, that they have received their orders from those before themselves and that this is the will of God. Clement also mentions that the apostles appointed their successors after first testing them by the spirit before ordaining them as bishops and deacons. This lends support to the idea that the disciples of the apostles carry some authority, thus giving weight to their word. Clement then goes on to say that: "Since all these things are clear to us, and we have looked into the depths of divine knowledge, we ought in proper order to do all things which the Lord has commanded us to perform at appointed times. He has commanded us the offerings and ministrations to be carried out, and not carelessly or disorderly, but at fixed times and seasons. For the High

Priest has been allotted his proper ministrations, and to the priests their proper place has been assigned, and on the levites their own duties are laid. The lay man is bound by lay ordinances." (*Letter to the Corinthians, Ch. 40*)

What a fascinating glimpse into the early church practices and a clear view of its hierarchal structure. Clement tells us that there is an orderly and careful way in which Christ has commanded them to perform ministrations and offerings, both references to the liturgical calendar and worship. Interestingly enough, Clement teaches that Christ commanded this structured form of worship, yet this is not found in scripture. Therefore Clement is referring to apostolic Tradition, which was passed on by word of mouth, and not scripture alone. Clement describes the same liturgical calendar, liturgical worship, and the hierarchal structure of the early church, which Orthodoxy practices to this day. When held to the mirror that is the early church, Orthodoxy is the reflection. It has an apostolic hierarchal structure, liturgical calendar, and liturgical worship, are all apostolic in origin. Clement then writes: "Our apostles also knew, through our Lord Jesus Christ, that there would be contention over the bishops office. So, for this cause, having received complete foreknowledge, they appointed the above mentioned men, and afterwards gave them a permanent character, so that, as they died, other approved men should succeed their ministry. Those, therefore, who were appointed by the apostles or afterwards by other eminent men, with the consent of the whole church, and who ministered blamelessly to the flock of Christ in humility, peaceably and nobly, being commended for many years by all. These men we consider are not justly deposed from their ministry." (*Letter to the Cortinthians, Ch. 44*)

Again Clement is speaking on the hierarchal structure and authority of the church. What is most interesting about this particular passage is his mention of the foreknowledge given to the apostles. According to Clement, Christ had taught the apostles things not contained in scripture. Christ gave His apostles foreknowledge, and established His church that would be in no need of a protestant style reformation, as it was established by Christ with this foreknowledge. In essence, this church would be in no need of new doctrines or practices. Clement lends support to this when he admonishes the Corinthians in saying: "It is disgraceful, very disgraceful and unworthy of your training in Christ, to hear that the stable and ancient church of the Corinthians, on account of one or two persons, should revolt against its presbyters. And this report has come not only to us, but also to those who dissent from us. The result is that blasphemies are brought upon the name of the Lord through your folly, and danger accrues for yourselves." (*Letter to the Corinthians, Ch.47*)

Clement harshly chastises the Corinthians for being rebellious against their presbyters. He equates this rebellion to blasphemy, urging them to repent stating that: "danger accrues for yourselves." Clement reveals to us that the priesthood is considered a sacred institution, so sacred that rebelling against it is akin to rebelling against God. Not only is this wrong, it is not considered Christian behavior. Clement sternly warns the Corinthians that this rebellion against the priesthood is dangerous. Ignatius of Antioch lends his support to this in his writings, saying that: "I exhort you to be careful to do all things in the harmony of God, the bishop having the primacy after the model of God and the priests after the model of the council of the apostles, and the deacons (who are so dear to me) having entrusted to them the ministry of Jesus Christ, who from eternity was with the father and at last appeared to us." (*Letter to the Magnesians, Ch.6*)

## **St. Clement of Alexandria**

To demonstrate consistency in practice and theology across time and space. What St. Ignatius taught in Antioch was taught in Rome and Alexandria. Clement teaches on the Eucharist saying: "Eat my flesh," [Jesus] says, "and drink my blood." The Lord supplies us with these intimate nutrients. He delivers over his flesh and pours out his blood, and nothing is lacking for the growth of his children. (*Paidagogos 1:6; 43:3*) - Clement of Alexandria. Also: "The young brood which the Lord Himself brought forth with throes of the flesh, which the Lord Himself swaddled with precious blood. O holy birth, O holy swaddling clothes, the Word is all to the babe, father and mother and tutor and nurse. "Eat ye My flesh," He says, "and drink ye My blood." (*Clement of Alexandria, Paed I:vi:42,43" vol 1, pg 37-38*)

Clement of Alexandria also referred to "bishops, presbyters, deacons" as "grades here in the Church" (*Strom., VI.13*) He then says: "God's "peculiar services," he writes, "are assigned to the high priest, and their own proper place is prescribed to the priests, and their own special ministrations devolve on the Levites. The layman is bound by the laws that pertain to laymen" (1 Cl. 40:5) fortieth chapter of his letter to the Corinthians)

Now we shall take a look at the fathers who came after St. Clement of Rome, St. Ignatius of Antioch, and St. Clement of Alexandria to demonstrate that even after them there was a continuity of teaching. There are a host of fathers who could be used here but that itself could be made into a book. For that reason we have chosen a select few of the early fathers to demonstrate this.

# St. Justin the Martyr

## Sacraments

"And the offering of fine flour, sirs, I said, which was prescribed to be presented on behalf of those purified from leprosy, was a type of the bread of the Eucharist, the celebration of which our Lord Jesus Christ prescribed, in remembrance of the suffering which He endured on behalf of those who are purified in soul from all iniquity. Hence God speaks by the mouth of Malachi, one of the twelve prophets as

I said before, about the sacrifices at that time presented by you: 'I have no pleasure in you, says the Lord; and I will not accept your sacrifices at your hands: for, from the rising of the sun unto the going down of the same, My name is great among the Gentiles, says the Lord: but you profane it'" (Dialogue with Trypho, Ch. 41)

"As many as are presuaded and believe that what we teach and say is true, and undertake to be able to live accordingly, are instructed to pray and to entreat God with fasting, for the remission of their sins that are past, we praying and fasting with them. They then are brought by us where there is water and are regenerated in the same manner in which we were ourselves regenerated. For, in the name of God, the Father and Lord of the universe, and of our Savior Jesus Christ, and of the Holy Spirit, they then receive the washing with water. The reason for this we have received from the Apostles. (First Apology, Ch. 61)

# St. Irenaeus

## Church Authority

"Since therefore we have such proofs, it is not necessary to seek the truth among others which it is easy to obtain from the Church; since the apostles, like a rich man [depositing his money] in a bank, lodged in her hands the most copiously all things pertaining to the truth: so that every man, whosoever will, can draw from her the water of life. For she is the entrance to life; all others are thieves and robbers. On this account we are bound to avoid them, but to make choice of the things pertaining to the Church with the utmost diligence, and to lay hold of the tradition of the truth. For how stands the case? Suppose there arise a dispute relative to some important questions among us, should we not have recourse to the most ancient Churches with which the apostles held constant communication, and learn from them what is certain and clear in regard to the present question? For how should it be if the apostles themselves had not left us writings? Would it not be necessary to follow the course of the tradition which they handed down to those to whom they did commit the churches?" (Against Heresies, Bk. 3, Ch. 4)

"Therefore it is necessary to obey the presbyters who are in the Church, those who, as I have shown, possess the succession from the apostles; those who, together with the succession of the episcopate, have received the certain gift of truth, according to the good pleasure of the Father. But it is also necessary to hold in suspicion others who depart from the primitive succession, and assemble themselves together in any place whatsoever." (Against Heresies, Bk. 4, Ch. 26)

"It is within the power of all, therefore, in every Church, who may wish to see the truth, to contemplate clearly the tradition of the apostles manifested throughout the whole world; and we are in a position to reckon up those who were by the apostles instituted bishops in the Churches, and to demonstrate the succession of these men to our own times; those who neither taught nor knew of anything like what these heretics rave about. For if the apostles had known hidden mysteries, which they were in the habit of imparting to 'the perfect' apart and privately from the rest, they would have delivered them especially to those to whom they were also committing the Churches themselves." ( Against Heresies Bk. 3, Ch. 3)

## **Sacraments**

"Again, giving directions to His disciples to offer to God the first fruits of His own created things, not as if He stood in need of them, but that they might be themselves neither unfruitful nor ungrateful. He took that created thing, bread, and gave thanks, and said, 'This is My Body' (Mt. 26:26). And the cup likewise which is part of that creation to which we belong, He confessed to be His blood, and taught the new oblation of the new covenant; which the Church receiving from the apostles, offers to God throughout all the world, to Him who gives us as the means of subsistence the first fruits of His own gifts in the New Testament, concerting which Malachi, among the twelve prophets, thus spoke beforehand: 'I have no pleasure in you, says the Lord Omnipotent, and I will not accept sacrifice at your hands. For from the rising of the sun, unto the going down of the same, My name is glorified among the Gentiles, and in every place incense is offered to My name, and a pure sacrifice; for great is My name among the Gentiles, said the Lord Omnipotent' (Mal. 1:10) - indicating in the plainest manner, by these words, that the former people, the Jews, shall indeed cease to make offerings to God, but that in every place sacrifice shall be offered to Him, and that a pure one; and His name be glorified among the Gentiles." (Against Heresies, Bk. 4, Ch. 17)

"Moreover, how could the Lord, with any justice, if He belonged to another father, have acknowledged the bread to be His body, while He took it from creation to which we belong, and affirmed the mixed cup to be His blood?" (Against Heresies, Bk. 4, Ch. 33)

# St. Cyprian

## Church Authority

"This unity we ought to hold firmly and defend, especially we bishops who watch over the church, that we may prove that also the episcopate itself is one and undivided. Let no one deceive the brotherhood by lying; let no one corrupt the faith by a perfidious prevarication of the truth. The episcopate is one, the parts of which are held together by the individual bishops. The church is one which with increasing fecundity extends far and wide into the multitude, just as the rays of the sun are many but the light is one, and the branches of the tree are many but the strength is one founded in its tenacious root, and, when many streams flow from one source, although a multiplicity of waters seems to have been diffused from abundance of the overflowing supply nevertheless unity is preserved in their origin. Take away a ray of light from the body of the sun, its unity does not take on any division of its light; break a branch from a tree, the branch thus broken will not be able to bud; cut off a stream from its source, the stream thus cut off dries up. Thus too the church bathed in the light of the Lord projects its rays over the whole world, yet there is one light which is diffused everywhere, and the unity of the body is not separated. She extends her branches over the whole earth in fruitful abundance; she extends her richly flowing streams far and wide; yet her head is one and her source is one, and she is the one mother copious in the results of her fruitfulness. By her womb we are born; by her milk we are nourished; by her spirit we are animated." (On the Unity of the Church, Ch. 5)

"The spouse of Christ cannot be defiled; she is uncorrupted and chaste. She knows one home, with chaste modesty she guards the sanctity of one couch. She keeps us for God; she assigns the children whom she has created to the kingdom. Whoever is separated from the Church and is joined with an adulteress is separated from the promises of the Church, nor will he who has abandoned the Church arrive at the rewards of Christ. He is a stranger; he is profane; he is an enemy. He cannot have God as a father who does not have the Church as a mother. If whoever was outside the ark of Noah was able to escape, he too who is outside the church escapes. The Lord warns, saying: 'He who is not with me is against me, and who does not gather with me, scatters.' He who breaks the peace and concord of Christ acts against Christ; he who gathers somewhere outside the Church scatters the Church of Christ. The Lord says: 'I and the Father are one' (Jn. 10:30). And again of the Father and Son and the Holy Spirit it is written: 'And these three are one' (Jn 5:7). Does anyone believe that this unity which comes from divine strength, which is closely connected with the divine sacraments, can be broken asunder in the Church and be separated by the divisions of colliding wills? He who does not hold this unity, does not hold the law of God, does not hold the faith of the Father and the Son, does not hold life and salvation. (On the Unity of the Church, Ch. 6)

## Sacraments

"In the sacraments of salvation, when necessity compels, and God bestows His mercy, the divine methods confer the whole benefit on believers; nor ought it to trouble anyone that sick people seem to be sprinkled or effused, when they obtain the Lord's grace" (Letters, No. 69:12)

"For although in smaller sins, sinners may do penance for a set time, and according to the rules of discipline come to public confession, and by imposition of the hand of the bishop and clergy receive the right of communion: now with their time still unfulfilled, while persecution is still raging, while the peace of the Church itself is not yet restored, they are admitted to communion, and their name is presented; and while the penance is not yet performed, confession is not yet made, the hands of the bishop and clergy are not yet laid upon them, the Eucharist is given to them; although it is written, Whoseover shall eat the bread and drink the cup of the Lord unworthily, shall be guilty of the body and blood of the Lord." (Letters, No. 16:2)

"It is also necessary that he should be anointed who is baptized; so that, having received the chrism, that is, the anointing, he may be anointed of God, and have in him the grace of Christ. Further, it is the Eucharist whence the baptized are anointed with the oil sanctified on the altar. But he cannot sanctify the creature of oil, who has neither an altar no a church; whence also there can be no spiritual anointing among heretics, since it is manifest that the oil cannot be sanctified nor the Eucharist celebrated at all among them." (Letters, No. 70:2

# **Mt 16:18**

We have demonstrated what is Christian by referring to the writings of St. Ignatius based on Acts 11:26, and St. Clement of Rome, St. Clement of Alexandria and St. Justin the Martyr, but how do we know which church is directly tied to the apostolic church? According to Mt. 16:18 Christ says: *"And I say also unto thee, That thou art Peter, and upon this rock I will build my church; and the gates of hell shall not prevail against it."* Logically we can conclude that His church that He founded should still be here from then, so how do we know which church, of the 38,000 some odd denominations, it is? Using the logic of the Acts 11:26 argument, we should trace the origins of the church to the present. We could start with Antioch, trace its origins to the present time by way of the patriarchs of the see of Antioch.

# List of Orthodox Patriarchs of Antioch

1. Peter the Apostle (ca. 37–ca. 53)

2. Evodius (ca. 53–ca. 69)

3. Ignatius (ca. 70–ca. 107)

4. Heron (107–127)

5. Cornelius (127–154)

6. Eros (154–169)

7. Theophilus (ca. 169–ca. 182)

8. Maximus I of Antioch (182–191)

9. Serapion (191–211)

10. Asclepiades the Confessor (211–220)

11. Philetus (220–231)

12. Zebinnus (231–237)

13. Babylas the Martyr (237–ca. 250).

14. Fabius (253–256)

15. Demetrius (ca. 256–uncertain)

16. Paul of Samosata (260–268)

17. Domnus I (268/9–273/4)

18. Timaeus (273/4–282)

19. Cyril I (283–303)

20. Tyrannion (304–314)

21. Vitalius (314–320)

22. Philogonius (320–323)

23. Eustathius (324–330)

24. Paulinus (330, six months)

25. Eulalius (331–332)

26. Euphronius (332–333)

27. Flacillus or Facellius (333–342)

28. Stephanus I of Antioch (342–344)

29. Leontius the Eunuch (344–358)

30. Eudoxius (358–359)

31. Anianus (359)

32. Meletius (360—361)

33. Paulinus (362–388)

34. Evagrius (388–393)

35. Theodotus (417–428)

36. John I (428–442)

37. Domnus II (442–449)

38. Maximus (449–455)

39. Basil of Antioch (456–458)

40. Acacius of Antioch (458–461)

41. Martyrius (461–469)

42. Peter the Fuller (469/470-471)

43. Julian (471–476)

44. Peter the Fuller (476)

45. John II Codonatus (476–477)

46. Stephanus II (477–479)

47. Calendion (479–485)

48. Peter the Fuller (485–488)

49. Palladius (488–498)

50. Flavian II (498–512)

51. Severus (512–538)

52. Sergius of Tella (544–546)

Vacant (546–550)

53. Paul II (550–575)

54. Theophanius (575-581)

55. Peter III (581–591)

56. Julian I (591–595)

57. Athanasius I Gammolo (595–631)

58. John II (631–648)

59. Theodore (649–667)

60. Severus II bar Mashqe (667–681)

61. Athanasius II (683–686)

62. Julian II (686–708)

63. Elias I (709–723)

64. Athanasius III (724–740)

65. Iwannis I (740–754)

66. Euwanis I (754–756)

67. Athanasius Sandalaya (756–758)

68. George I (758–790)

69. Joseph (790–792)

70. Quriaqos of Tagrit (793–817)

71. Dionysius I of Tel Mahre (817–845)

72. John III (846–873)

73. Ignatius II (878–883)

74. Theodosius Romanos of Takrit (887–896)

75. Dionysius II (897–909)

76. John IV Qurzahli (910–922)

77. Baselius I (923–935)

78. John V (936–953)

79. Iwanis II (954–957)

80. Dionysius III (958–961)

81. Abraham I (962–963)

82. John VI Sarigta (965–985)

83. Athanasius IV of Salah (986–1002)

84. John VII bar Abdun (1004–1033)

85. Dionysius IV Yahya (1034–1044)

Vacant (1044–1049)

86. John VIII (1049–1057)

87. Athanasius V (1058–1063)

88. John IX bar Shushan (1063–1073)

89. Baselius II (1074–1075)

90. John Abdun (1075–1077)

91. Dionysius V Lazaros (1077–1078)

92. Iwanis III (1080–1082)

Vacant (1082–1088)

93. Dionysius VI (1088–1090)

94. Athanasius VI bar Khamoro (1091–1129)

95. John X bar Mawdyono (1129–1137)

96. Athanasius VII bar Qutreh (1138–1166)

97. Michael the Great (1166–1199)

98. Athanasius VIII (1200–1207)

99. John XI (1208–1220)

Vacant (1220–1222)

100. Ignatius III David (1222–1252)

101. John XII bar Madani (1252–1263)

102. Ignatius IV Yeshu (1264–1282)

103. Philoxenos I Nemrud (1283–1292)

104. Michael II (1292–1312)

105. Michael III Yeshu (1312–1349)

106. Baselius III Gabriel (1349–1387)

107. Philoxenos II (1387–1421)

108. Baselius IV Shemun (1421–1444)

109. Ignatius Behnam alHadli (1445–1454)

110. Ignatius Khalaf (1455–1483)

111. Ignatius John XIV (1483–1493)

112. Ignatius Nuh of Lebanon (1493–1509)

113. Ignatius Yeshu I (1509–1512)

114. Ignatius Jacob I (1512–1517)

115. Ignatius David I (1517–1520)

116. Ignatius AbdAllah I (1520–1557)

117. Ignatius Nemet Allah I (1557–1576)

118. Ignatius David II Shah (1576–1591)

119. Ignatius Pilate I (1591–1597)

120. Ignatius Hadayat Allah (1597–1639)

121. Ignatius Simon I (1640–1659)

122. Ignatius Yeshu II Qamsheh (1659–1662)

123. Ignatius Abdul Masih I (1662–1686)

124. Ignatius George II (1687–1708)

125. Ignatius Isaac Azar (1709–1722)

126. Ignatius Shukr Allah II (1722–1745)

127. Ignatius George III (1745–1768)

128. Ignatius George IV (1768–1781)

129. Ignatius Matthew (1783–1817)

130. Ignatius Yunan (1817–1818)

131. Ignatius George V (1819–1837)

132. Ignatius Elias II (1838–1847)

133. Ignatius Jacob II (1847–1871)

134. Ignatius Peter IV (1872–1894)

135. Ignatius Abdul Masih II (1895–1905)

136. Ignatius Abded Aloho II (1906–1915)

137. Ignatius Elias III (1917–1932)

138. Ignatius Afram I Barsoum (1933–1957)

139. Ignatius Jacob III (1957–1980)

140. Ignatius Zakka I (1980–2014)

141. Ignatius Aphrem II (2014–present) [3,4,5,6]


From St. Peter the Apostle to Ignatius Aphrem II we have an unbroken apostolic line from the apostles to the present day. This is called apostolic succession from one patriarch to the next in a continual unbroken line of succession, keeping the teaching of the church intact. This is how every Orthodox church establishes its legitimacy, by tracing itself to the apostles, without this anyone can claim authority. This echoes the words of Christ in Mt. 23 when He says: "The scribes and the Pharisees sit in Moses' seat: all therefore whatsoever they bid you observe, that observe and do; but do not ye after their works: for they say, and do not." Christ is hinting at this successive authority when referring to the pharisees sitting on Moses' seat, much like the patriarchs of today sitting on the seat of the apostles. The Coptic Orthodox Church of Alexandria is another of the ancient churches which can trace its roots back to Christ through St. Mark the evangelist. He founded the church in about 43 a.d.

## List of Coptic Orthodox Patriarchs

1. Mark the Evangelist (43–68)

2. Anianus (68–82)

3. Avilius (83–95)

4. Kedron (96–106)

5. Primus (106–118)

6. Justus (118–129)

7. Eumenes (131–141)

8. Markianos (142–152)

9. Celadion (152–166)

10. Agrippinus (167–178)

11. Julian (178–189)

12. Demetrius I (189–232)

13. Heraclas (232–248)

14. Dionysius (248–264)

15. Maximus (265–282)

16. Theonas (282–300)

17. Peter I (300–311)

18. Achillas (312–313)

19. Alexander I (313–326)

vacant (326–328)

20. Athanasius I (328–373)

21. Peter II (373–380)

22. Timothy I (380–385)

23. Theophilus I (385–412)

24. Cyril I (412–444)

25. Dioscorus I (444–454)

vacant (454–457)

26.Timothy II Aelurus (457–477)

27. Peter III Mongus (477–490)

28. Athanasius II (490–496)

29. John I (496–505)

30. John II (505–516)

31. Dioscorus II (516–517)

32. Timothy III (517–535)

33. Theodosius I (535–567)

34. Peter IV (567–569)

35. Damian (569–605)

36. Anastasius (605–616)

37. Andronicus (616–622)

38. Benjamin I (622–661) Islam entered Egypt

39. Agatho (661–677)

40. John III (677–688)

41. Isaac (688–689)

42. Simeon I (689–701)

43. Alexander II (702–729)

44. Cosmas I (729–730)

45. Theodosius II (730–742)

46. Michael I (743–767)

47. Mina I (767–775)

48. John IV (776–799)

49. Mark II (799–819)

50. Jacob (819–830)

51. Simeon II (830)

52. Joseph I (831–849)

53. Michael II (849–851)

54. Cosmas II (851–858)

55. Shenouda I (859–880)

56. Michael III (880–907)

vacant (907–910)

56. Gabriel I (910–921)

58. Cosmas III (921–933)

59. Macarius I (933–953)

60. Theophilus II (953–956)

61. Mina II (956–974)

62. Abraham (975–978)

63. Philotheos (979–1003)

64. Zacharias (1004–1032)

65. Shenouda II (1032–1046)

66. Christodolos (1047–1077)

67. Cyril II (1078–1092)

68. Michael IV (1092–1102)

69. Macarius II (1102–1131)

70. Gabriel II (1131–1145)

71. Michael V (1145–1146)

72. John V (1147–1166)

73. Mark III (1166–1189)

74. John VI (1189–1216)

vacant (1216–1235)

75. Cyril III (1235–1243)

vacant (1243–1250)

76. Athanasius III (1250–1261)

77. John VII (1262–1268)

78. Gabriel III (1268–1270)

79. John VII (restored) (1270–1293)

80. Theodosius III (1293–1300)

81. John VIII (1300–1320)

82. John IX (1320–1327)

83. Benjamin II (1327–1339)

84. Peter V (1340–1348)

85. Mark IV (1348–1363)

86. John X (1363–1369)

87. Gabriel IV (1370–1378)

88. Matthew I (1378–1408)

89. Gabriel V (1408–1427)

90. John XI (1427–1452)

91. Matthew II (1453–1466)

92. Gabriel VI (1466–1475)

93. Michael VI (1475–1477)

94. John XII (1480–1483)

95. John XIII (1483–1524)

vacant (1524–1526)

96. Gabriel VII (1526–1569)

vacant (1569–1573)

97. John XIV (1573–1589)

98. Gabriel VIII (1587–1603)

vacant (1603–1610)

99. Mark V (1610–1621)

100. John XV (1621–1631)

101. Matthew III (1631–1645)

102. Mark VI (1645–1660)

103. Matthew IV (1660–1676)

104. John XVI (1676–1718)

105. Peter VI (1718–1726)

106. John XVII (1727–1745)

107. Mark VII (1745–1769)

108. John XVIII (1769–1796)

109. Mark VIII (1797–1810)

110. Peter VII (1810–1852)

vacant (1852–1854)

111. Cyril IV (1854–1861)

112. Demetrius II (1862–1870)

vacant (1870–1874)

113. Cyril V (1874–1927)

114. John XIX (1928–1942)

vacant (1942–1944)

115. Macarius III (1944–1945)

vacant (1945–1946)

116. Joseph II (1946–1956)

vacant (1956–1959)

117. Cyril VI (1959–1971)

118. Shenouda III (1971-2012)

119. Tawadros II (2012 - present) [7,8,9]


Here we have two apostolic churches that can trace their roots back to Christ through the apostles. This shows that when Christ says His church will not be overcome, that it should still be here and those that *can* demonstrate their apostolic link are the church that Christ established through His disciples and apostles. Subsequently following this Christ tells his followers that "And I will give you the keys of the kingdom of heaven, and whatever you bind on earth will be bound in heaven, and whatever you loose on earth will be loosed in heaven." (*Mt. 16:19, Jn 20:23*) This shows that the followers of Christ were given special authority, now, did that authority die with the apostles or was this authority passed on to their successors? Well, if they were given power to forgive sins then it stands to reason that they would pass this authority of Christ on to their successors. Otherwise it was only the apostles who were given the authority of Christ to forgive sins and it died with them. So it was clearly important enough for Christ to give them this authority but why let it die with the apostles if its that important? It stands to reason that it was likely passed on thereby giving more weight to apostolic succession. Binding and loosing is a reference to the teaching, sacramental, and administrative powers of the apostles, which were passed on to the Bishops. This is also a reference to forgiving and retaining sins, as seen in John 20:23. This passing down of authority is a constant cycle that has continued for centuries, called Apostolic Succession.

" I will give you the keys of the kingdom of heaven..." What a peculiar statement, and very confusing to those without the church as their mother. The Orthodox faithful should know and understand this very well because Christ is referring to the Divine Liturgy, as this is heavenly worship in God's kingdom, as detailed in Rev. 8: " When the Lamb opened the seventh seal, there was a silence in heaven for about half an hour. Then I saw the seven angels who stand before God, and seven trumpets were given to them. And another angel came and stood at the altar with a golden censer, and he was given much incense to offer with the prayers of all the saints on the golden altar before the throne, and the smoke of the incense, with the prayers of the saints, rose before God from the hand of the angel." So here we see graphically that the keys to the kingdom are the keys to the heavenly worship, the divine

liturgy, which is taking place in heaven as detailed above

## <u>εκκλησία (ekklesia) and קהל (qahal)</u>

If we first start with a modern word study on ekklesia,

we must naturally begin with the secular meaning of the

Greek, that it was a group of citizens which had been called

together. The goal of this study however, is to arrive at the

meaning of the word as used in the Gospel of Matthew. The

first time it is spoken in the New Testament, by Christ, is at

Matthew 16:18, "…And I say also unto thee, That thou art

Peter, and upon this rock I will build my ekklesia" One of the

important parts of any scriptural doctrine is the words which

the authors selected to name or describe that

particular doctrine. The doctrine of the Lord's church, or

Ecclesiology, derives its name from the Greek word ekklesia

( ekklhsia ). A proper understanding of that word is essential to

a proper understanding of Ecclesiology.

The most common classical usage of ekklesia and its cognates was as a political term, meaning an assembly of citizens. In the Greece, citizens were called by the heralds trumpet summoning them to the ekklesia (assembly). The ekklesia was the seat power in the Greek city-state. Aristotle later applied the term ekklesiai to the Homeric assemblies of the people. Most of our references to the use of this word concern the ekklesiai of Athens. The ekklesia in Athens lasted from 508 B.C. until the early fourth century, A.D. During its span, it was the general meeting of the people. All Athenian citizens were permitted and encouraged to attend, excluding only aliens, females, and those that had been expelled. By law the ekklesia had to be summoned at least four times each 36 or 37 days, that is, forty times each year. One of each four meetings was considered to be of greater importance than the others, and it was called the ekklesiakuria. Any citizen was permitted to speak in debate and initiate amendments or administrative motions. Voting was normally by show of hands, a simple majority deciding most issues. In its ordinary

usage, ekklesia referred to the assembly, and not to the people

involved. There was a new ekklesia every time they

assembled. An ekklesia was "called forth" for a specific

purpose; it was not just any gathering of people. The word

ekkletos (ekklhtoj), an adjective also derived from ekkaleo,

may serve to illustrate this. A person described as ekkletos was

someone selected to judge or render a decision. Xenophon, the

ancient Greek historian, describes a group called on to render a

decision about the requests of some ambassadors during a time

of civil war. He describes this group as ekkletos. In like

manner an ekklesia was summoned because decisions or

judgments had to be made.

## Jewish Usage:

Root QHL (קהל) qahal is translated into English

as multitude, company, congregation, and assembly. Ekklesia

occurs eighty times in the Septuagint translation (LXX) of the

Old Testament, and where the Hebrew original is available for comparison, it always uses this word, qahal (קהל) or some variation of the word stemming from the same root. This term was used in the Old Testament to denote a gathering or assembly: qahal and the term qahal denoted not the people themselves, but rather the actual assembly or meeting. Though ekklesia is nearly always a translation of qahal, on the other hand, qahal is also translated by other Greek words, in particular, synagogue. In thirty five passages synagogue is used in place of qahal, nineteen of these passages being in the first four books where ekklesia is never used. In the light of this study of the existing evidence concerning the pre-Christian history of ekklesia, it is logical to conclude: (1) Ekklesia meant an assembly. (2) It was familiar both to Gentiles by political usage and to Greek-speaking Jews through the LXX. (3) Its Greek history associated with it a certain dignity, with possible ideals of freedom and equal-membership playing a part. (4) It could be used of a religious assembly; Pagan or Jewish, but it did not become the title of any religious group, Pagan or Jewish.

## Historian Usage:

Philo (A.D. 39) uses ekklesia 30 times: five as in classical Greek, and twenty five in LXX quotations, especially from Deuteronomy 23. He sometimes qualifies ekklesia by an adjective: theia or hiera; and he also uses it with the genitives theou and kuriou. In these passages there is no evidence whatsoever that the word alone has a distinct religious connotation. On occasions he uses sullogos interchangeably with ekklesia, and he modifies this word by hieros. There is one passage where Philo might have used ekklesia in a technical sense. "For when the whole multitude came together with harmonious oneness to give thanks for their migration, He no longer called them a multitude or a nation or a people but a 'congregation'." Josephus (37-c. 100 A.D.) used the term ekklesia forty eight times, all according to strict classical usage. Eighteen of these passages may represent LXX allusions, and in nine cases he substitutes ekklesia for synagogue.

## Early Church Usage:

Ekklesia occurs one hundred fourteen times in the New Testament, being found in Matthew, Acts, Romans, 1 Corinthians, 2 Corinthians, Galatians, Ephesians, Philippians, Colossians, 1 Thessalonians, 2 Thessalonians, 1 Timothy, Philemon, Hebrews, James, 3 John, and Revelation. Its use, however, differs strongly from what we have seen from pre-Christian history. Although ekklesia at times denotes an actual assembly, in general there is a real sense in which the ekklesia exists whether it is physically assembled or not. This is not a development which can be detected prior to Christian history, and the change is probably to be explained as a strictly Christian phenomenon. Epiphanius states that the Ebionite Christians used synagogue instead of ekklesia. But synagogue had by the first century, A.D., assumed too much of a technical status, denoting the religious assemblies of the Jews, these Jews themselves, and the places where they assembled. But ekklesia was not tied down to any group, much less to a religious group. Though used in the LXX, it was not distinct only to the Jewish people, rather it was a term applied by Jew and Gentile alike.

Ekklesia is used twenty three times by the author of Acts. In two instances (19:32,40) it refers to the mob of people at Ephesus. In this passage it is also used to refer to the assembly which met regularly (ennomoi) at Ephesus (19:39). Once ekklesia is used in the speech of Stephen (7 :38) to designate the children of Israel gathered at Sinai, echoing perhaps Deuteronomy 9:10 where the LXX has ekklesia. In the passages which remain, ekklesia refers to the institution of Jesus Christ. It most closely resembles classical usage in 14:27 where the assembly is actually gathered at Antioch to listen to the teaching of Paul and Barnabas. In the rest, ekklesia means more than the actual assembly; it is also the people who assemble. As the author writes: "great fear came upon the whole church" in Jerusalem (*5: 11*) ; there is a "great persecution of the church in Jerusalem" (8:1) and "Saul was laying waste the church, entering in house to house" (8:3).

In every case, with one possible exception, ekklesia. is explicitly or implicitly used in a physical sense: it is the assembly (assembled or not) at Jerusalem (*11:22; 12:1, 5; 15:4, 22*), at Antioch (*11:26; 13:1;14:27; 15:3*), at Caesarea (*18:22*), and at Ephesus (*20:17,28*). This local use is emphasized by the use of the plural, ekklesiai, when referring to churches in a larger area: in Syria and Cilicia (15 :41) and in areas of Asia Minor (16:4). The only possible exception to the physical use is found in Acts 9 :31: "So then the Church throughout all Judea and Galilee and Samaria had peace, having been strengthened."

Ekklesia is used sixty two times in the Pauline epistles. In Paul's first letter to Corinth he uses ekklesia several times according to common usage; denoting an actual assembly:

"For first when you have come together in an assembly, I hear there are divisions among you" (*11:18; see also14:19, 28, 35*). The ekklesia is more often than not referred to as physical and tied to a locality: the church at Cenchreae (Romans 16:1), I at Corinth (*1 Corinthians 1:2; 2 Corinthians 1:1*), at Laodicea (*Colossians 4:16*), and at Thessalonica (*1 Thessalonians 1:1; 2 Thessalonians 1:1*). When speaking of a larger geographical area Paul uses the plural: the churches of Asia (*1 Corinthians 16:19*), of Galatia (*1 Corinthians 16:1; Galatians 1:1*), of Macedonia (*2 Cointhians. 8:1*), of Judea (*Galatians1:22; 1 Thessalonians 2:14*). Paul also uses ekklesia of smaller groups, such as the household church of Prisea and Aquila in Rome (*Romans 16:5*), that of the same couple in Ephesus (*1 Corinthians 16:19*), that of Nympha in Laodicea (*Colossians. 4:15*) and that of Philemon in Colosse (*Philemon 2*). These can evidently be called ekklesia, even while calling the total group in the city ekklesia.

It is in Paul's letters to the Ephesians and Colossians that ekklesia receives its fullest expression, and at the same time is removed the furthest from its classical usage. But the term itself remained nonetheless, neutral rather than expressive of the doctrine concerning that institution. This being so, the classical meaning of assembly, gathering has been superseded by the more dynamic, Pauline definition: ekklesia being the body of Christ, or even, Christ himself!

Ekklesia by name is found in only one of the four gospels, Matthew, and in only two passages in that gospel (*16:18; 18: 17*). Recent scholarship has asserted that the ekklesia is an integral part of the teaching of Jesus. The question remains as to why ekklesia is scarcely used in the gospels. This term seems to be generally reserved for the time after the resurrection and the ascension of Jesus as the Christ. Matthew 16:18. Many problems exist concerning this passage, but most importantly, if ekklesia means only a physical assembly, then the statement here: "Upon this rock I will build my 'meeting' (ekklesia)" is empty of any real meaning.

Matthew 18: 17. The two occasions of ekklesia in this passage must be understood in its common usage: as an actual assembly. And that assembly is, no doubt, present rather than future, Jewish rather than Christian.

## Peshitta Usage:

The possible Aramaic equivalents include: qehala', 'edutha', qibura', and kenushtha'. All four of these words are associated with the idea of the People of God. In the Peshitta, the most common of these terms is kenushtha, meaning gathering, assembly, place of meeting. Furthermore, the Sinaitic Syriac version (3rd century, A.D.) uses kenushtha regularly for ekklesia and synagogue, and the Palestinian Syriac version also uses kenushtha for both Greek words. Therefore, most linguists conclude that the word kenushtha would most closely represent the Aramaic equivalent.

Whether it was kenushtha or one of the other mentioned words, it would be meaningful here in this passage. Each would convey the idea of the People of God, an idea fully in keeping with the figure of "building," and each would be a term with Messianic overtones. Matthew later records his gospel in Greek using ekklesia as the natural translation of the Aramaic. Synagogue would have been eliminated as being a strictly Jewish term. But by Matthew's time ekklesia was the technical, religious term in usage to designate what Jesus had promised to build.[10-36]

## Mt. 7:22,23

*"Many will say to Me in that day, 'Lord, Lord, have we not prophesied in Your name, cast out demons in Your name, and done many wonders in Your name?' And then I will declare to them, I never knew you; depart from Me, you who practice lawlessness!"* What an amazing verse, one in which Christ accuses those that clearly consider themselves Christian of practicing lawlessness and to depart from Him for it. Logically we can conclude that if there is a way to practice

Christianity lawlessly, then there is a way in which to practice it lawfully. We could go directly to scripture, however, the issue with that is interpretation. These days everyone seems to have their own opinion as to what the bible really means and therefore to quote it would be pointless. We can solve this problem by referring back to St. Ignatius to see what being a Christian means based on Acts 11:26.

Assuming that St. Ignatius' teachings reflected that of the apostles that taught him, and we have no reason to assume otherwise, then it is clear what being a Christian means. The Christian church has a hierarchal structure, and one must obey the bishop because to obey him is to obey Christ. There is also the Eucharist and Baptism, which St. Ignatius says is not lawful for either to be done without the consent of the bishop. The Eucharist is considered to be the body and blood of Jesus Christ, not merely symbolic. He says, in fact, that the docetics do not receive communion because they deny that it is the body and blood of Jesus Christ, meaning clearly that this is not just symbolic but sacred and meant to be taken seriously.

St. Ignatius also says, in referring to clergy, that: "Apart from these there is nothing that can be called a church." Therefore it is lawless to practice apart from the bishop, priests, and deacons as St. Ignatius states that apart from them nothing can be called a church. Therefore those in Mt. 7:22,23 who practice lawlessness, practice apart from the bishop and or do not hold the sacraments, namely Baptism and the Eucharist, as being sacred but merely symbolic, if they practice them at all. What other law could Christ be referring to when accusing them of lawlessness? If there is lawlessness then there is law, if there is law then there is a law keeper as you cannot have law if there are not those who keep it so that others may know it. Without a law keeper there would be lawlessness, like those who choose to ignore the law keeper, are they not ignoring the law and the one who gave it?

In terms of practice we can also refer to the liturgy of St. James, the brother of Jesus Christ. This is the oldest form of Eastern varieties of the Divine Liturgy still in use today and is associated with St. James as having written it himself. While the date of its composition is still disputed, many authorities place the date to around 60 A.D. which means it was likely written during the time of the apostles. This liturgy has been in use since the earliest part of the Christian Church and thus demonstrates how the Eucharist was celebrated. Therefore when St. Ignatius refers to the Eucharist he is thereby indirectly referring to the liturgy.

We can also see the liturgy being practiced in heaven in Revelation 8: "*When He opened the seventh seal, there was silence in heaven for about half an hour. And I saw the seven angels who stand before God, and to them were given seven trumpets. Then another angel, having a golden censer, came and stood at the altar. He was given much incense, that he should offer it with the prayers of all the saints upon the golden altar which was before the throne. And the smoke of the incense, with the prayers of the saints, ascended before God from the angel's hand."* There we can see an altar, an angel acting as a priest with a censer and incense offering the incense with the prayers of the saints before God. This is a direct reference to the liturgy which is clearly practiced in heaven and therefore the lawful way in which to worship God.

## On Earth as it is in Heaven

How can we know for sure what is lawful and what is not in order to please Christ? To put it simply we must do the will of God, as stated in our Lords Prayer: "Your will be done on earth as it is in heaven." While this is undoubtedly true how are we to know what the will of God is? Can we know what is being done in heaven that we ought to do here on earth? One place that we clearly see what is taking place in heaven is in Revelation 8 where we are told: "And I saw the seven angels who stand before God, and to them were given seven trumpets. Then another angel, having a golden censer, came and stood at the altar. He was given much incense, that he should offer it with the prayers of all the saints upon the golden altar which was before the throne. And the smoke of the incense, with the prayers of the saints, ascended before God from the angel's hand."(Rev. 8:2-4)

What we see here is a distinct form of worship known as liturgical worship. We see an angel with a golden censer standing at an altar. He used incense to offer to God with the prayers of the saints, which is known as intercession. We do this very thing in Orthodoxy, liturgical worship. The priest stands before the altar and offers incense which rises up before God with the prayers of the saints. This is all a distinct form of worship called liturgical. This type of worship has been done since the foundation of Judaism and continued through the early church to now. It stands to reason that if we are to do the will of God, as is said in the Lord's prayer, then we should seek to do this form of worship here on earth as it is in heaven. Doing the will of God is what is lawful and as we seen in Mt. 7:22 we do not want to be the unlawful whom Christ sends away.

Liturgy would undoubtedly be the form of worship the apostles would be most familiar with as this is how the jews practiced, liturgically. Christ tells the apostles in Mt. 23 that: "The scribes and the Pharisees sit in Moses' seat. 3 Therefore whatever they tell you to observe, that observe and do, but do not do according to their works; for they say, and do not do." The jews manner of observing is through liturgy or the liturgical calendar which indicates that they would have continued this, since Christ did say that He did not come to abolish the law and the prophets but to fulfill (Mt. 5:17). Not only is liturgical worship being done in heaven but it is what Christ clearly instructed the apostles to observe.

# **Conclusion**

The conclusion I leave to the reader, for you to decide what the conclusion may be. I can further attempt to prove my point here or I can let the information sink in and leave it to the reader to decide what to conclude. I believe it is only honest and fair for me to prove my point as best I can and then step back and let you, the reader, ponder what has just been read and then conclude if I have sufficiently proven my point. And if I have, I leave it to you to do what you see fit with the information I have given you.

# Sources

1. Peterson J.B. Transcribed by Nicolette Ormsbee.The Apostolic Fathers. The Catholic Encyclopedia, Volume I. Copyright © 1907 by Robert Appleton Company. Online Edition Copyright © 2003 by K. Knight. Nihil Obstat, March 1, 1907. Remy Lafort, S.T.D., Censor. Imprimatur. +John Cardinal Farley, Archbishop of New York


2. Pope St. Clement I. The Catholic Encyclopedia, Volume IV. Copyright © 1908 by Robert Appleton Company. Online Edition Copyright © 2003 by K. Knight. Nihil Obstat. Remy Lafort, Censor. Imprimatur. +John M. Farley, Archbishop of New York


3. Walter Bauer, Greek-English Lexicon of the New Testament and Other Early Christian Literature, 2ed., 1979

4. de Boor, Carl, ed. (1880). Nicephori Archiepiscopi Constantinopolitani Opuscula Historica. Teubner (Leipzig, repr. NY, Arno Press, 1975) pp.129–132. ISBN 0-405-07177-9.

5. La Civita, Michael J.L. "Profiles of the Eastern churches: The Syriac Orthodox Church". www.cnewa.org. Catholic Near East Welfare Association.

6. Pour Un Oriens Christianus Novus: Repertoire Des Dioceses Syriaques Orientaux Et Occidentaux. Beirut: Steiner. pp. 275–277. ISBN 3-515-05718-8.

7. The Early Coptic Papacy: The Egyptian Church and Its Leadership in Late Antiquity (Popes of Egypt)
Stephen J. Davis

8. The Emergence of the Modern Coptic Papacy: The Popes of Egypt: A History of the Coptic Church and Its Patriarchs, Volume 3, Majd Jirjis

9. The Coptic Papacy in Islamic Egypt: The Popes of Egypt: A History of the Coptic Church and Its Patriarchs Volume 2 by Mark N. Swanson

10. The Misunderstanding of the Church (Translation by H. Knight, London: Luttenvorth Press, 1952), p. 10, etc.

11. Das Problem der Urkirche in der neueren Forshung (Uppsala Universitets Arsskrift, 1932) ; for more recent additions to this bibliography see W. Arndt [176] and F. Gingrich, A Greek-English Lexicon of the New Testament (Chicago: The University of Chicago Press, 1957).

12. Politics 1285a 11. 174 175

13. See references in Thuc., Herod., Aristoph., Plato., Arist., and in inscriptions and other non-literary sources.

14. A. W. Gomme, "Ecclesia," The Oxford Classical Dictionary, p. 304.

15. C. G. Brandis, "Ekklesia," Pauly's Real-Encyclopaedie der classischen altertumswissenschaft, revised by Wissowa, (1905), vol. 5, cols. 2163-2200; R. Whiston and W. Wayte, "Ecclesia," A Dictionary of Greek and Roman Antiquity, vol. 1, pp. 697-703.

16. Thuc. 3.46: en tei proterai ekklesiai (in the earlier assembly); inscription in Dittenberger,Sylloge Inscriptionum Graecarum, vol. 3, p. 101: en tei deuterai ton ekklesion (in the second of the assemblies).

17. Dittenberger, op. cit., vol. 3, p. 512:prosetaxen ho demos. . . (the people commanded) ; vol. 1, p. 731: psephisma tou demos (the vote of the people).

18. Liddell and Scott, A Greek-English Lexicon (Jones-McKenzie edition), S.v.

19. Aristotle, Politics, 1275b 8.

20. E. L. Hicks, "On Some Political Terms Employed in the New Testament," Classical Review, 1 (1887), p. 43. Moulton and Milligan cite as a non-literary example of the "inclusive" use of ekklesia the assembly at Apamea: agomenes pandemou ekklesias (being gathered in the assembly of all the people). The Vocabulary of the Greek New Testament, S.v.

21. F. J. A. Hort, The Christian Ecclesia (London: Macmillan and Co., 1898), p. 5.

22. J. Y. Campbell, "The Origin and Meaning of the Christian Use of the Word EKKLESIA,"Journal of Theological Studies, 49 (1948), p. 131.

23. A. Deissmann, Light From the Ancient East (New York: George H. Doran Co., 1927), p. 113.

24. Corpus Inscriptionum Graecarum, 2271. Geschichte des griechischen Vereinwesens (Leipzig: B. G. Teubner, 1909), p. 332.

25. Johan D. W. Kritzinger,Qehal Jahwe. Wat dit is en wie daaraan rna.q behoort (Acad. Proefschrift, Kampen: Kok, 1957),

26. L. Rost in Theologische Literaturzeitung, (1958), pp. 266, 267.

27. De Confusione Linguarum, 144.

28. Quod Deusimmutabilis sit, 111; De Migratione Abrahami, 69; De Somniis, ii, 184, 187.

29. Legum Allegoria, iii, 8.

30. De Ebrietate, 213.

31. Legum Allegoria, iii, 81; De Somniis, ii, 184; De Specialibus Legibus, i, 325.

32. Quaestiones et Solutiones in Exodum, 1.10, translated by Ralph Marcus in the Loeb Classical Library, supplement to Philo series, vol. 2, pp. 19, 20.

33. Philo Judaeus, Paralipomena Armena (Armenian text and Latin translation by P. Aucher, 1826), p. 456.

34. R. Newton Flew, Jesus and His Church (New York: The Abingdon Press, 1938); Schmidt, op. cit.; Johnston, op. cit.; Anders Nygren, Christ and His Church (translation by Carlsten, Philadelphia: The Westminster Press, 1956); and various works connected with the ecumenical movement.

35. Apostolic Constitutions II. 59; an edict of Maximmus (303-313 A.D.) in Eusebius, Eccl. Hist, ix. 10; canon 15 of the Council of Ancyra (314); canon 5 of the Council of Neo-Caesarea (314-323); canon 28 of the council of Laodicea.

36. "Church," A New English Dictionary on Historical Principles (edited by J. H. Murray, Oxford: Clarendon Press, 1893), vol. 2, pp. 402, 406.

www.ingramcontent.com/pod-product-compliance
Lightning Source LLC
Chambersburg PA
CBHW032209040426
42449CB00005B/514